P9-CAT-222

Colin Powell

By Mary Hill

Welcome Books™

Children's Press®
A Division of Scholastic Inc.
New York / Toronto / London / Auckland / Sydney
Mexico City / New Delhi / Hong Kong
Danbury, Connecticut

Photo Credits: Cover, pp. 13, 21 © AFP/Corbis; p. 5 © Joseph Sohm/Chromosohm Inc./Corbis; p. 19 © Rufus F. Folkks/Corbis; p. 7 © Peter Turnley/Corbis; p. 9 © Tim Shaffer/Reuters/TimePix; p. 11 © Reuters NewMedia Inc./Corbis; p. 15 © Wally McNamee/Corbis; p. 17 © AP/Wide World Photos
Contributing Editor: Jennifer Silate
Book Design: Daniel Hosek

Library of Congress Cataloging-in-Publication Data

Hill, Mary, 1977–
    Colin Powell / by Mary Hill.
    p. cm. — (Real people)
    Summary: An easy-to-read biography of General Colin Powell
    who, in 2001, became the first African American to be appointed
    secretary of state.
    Includes bibliographical references (p.) and index.
    ISBN 0-516-24288-1 (lib. bdg.) — ISBN 0-516-27885-1 (pbk.)
    1. Powell, Colin L.—Juvenile literature. 2. Statesmen—United
    States—Biography—Juvenile literature. 3. Generals—United
    States—Biography—Juvenile literature. 4. African American
    generals—Biography—Juvenile literature. 5. United States.
    Army—Biography—Juvenile literature. [1. Powell, Colin L. 2. Cabinet
    officers. 3. Generals. 4. African Americans—Biography.] I. Title. II.
    Series: Real people (Children's Press)

    E840.8.P64 H55 2003
    327.73'0092--dc21
                                                    2002152677

Contents

Meet Colin Powell.

Colin Powell worked for the United States of America.

5

Colin Powell was a **general** in the United States **Army**.

Colin was given many **awards** for his **bravery**.

In 2001, President George W. Bush chose Colin to be the **secretary of state**.

Colin Powell was the first **African American** to ever have that job.

Colin Powell visited many countries when he was secretary of state.

He met with the leaders of other countries.

13

Colin Powell also gave many **speeches** around the world.

He talked about making people's lives better.

15

Colin also worked with groups that help children.

17

Colin Powell is **married** to Alma Johnson.

Colin Powell worked hard to make the world a better place.

21

New Words

African American (**af**-ruh-kuhn uh-**mer**-uh-kuhn) someone who was born in the United States or became a U.S. citizen and can trace his or her ancestors back to Africa

army (**ar**-mee) a group of people who fight together during a war

awards (uh-**wordz**) prizes given to a person for doing something well

bravery (**brayv**-uhr-ee) strong and without fear

general (**jen**-ur-uhl) a very high-ranking officer in the army

married (**mar**-eed) having a husband or wife

secretary of state (**sek**-ruh-ter-ee **uhv stayt**) a person who advises the president of the United States on how to handle things with other countries

speeches (**speech**-uhz) talks given to groups of people

22

To Find Out More

Books
Colin Powell
by John Passaro
Childs World

Colin Powell: It Can Be Done!
by Mike Strong
Capstone Press

Web Site
General Powell's Corner
http://www.americaspromise.org/GenPowellCorner/
    GenPowellCorner.cfm
Read about Colin Powell and a letter he wrote to
the kids of America.

Index

About the Author
Mary Hill writes and edits children's books.

Reading Consultants
Kris Flynn, Coordinator, Small School District Literacy, The San Diego County Office of Education

Shelly Forys, Certified Reading Recovery Specialist, W.J. Zahnow Elementary School, Waterloo, IL

Sue McAdams, Former President of the North Texas Reading Council of the IRA, and Early Literacy Consultant, Dallas, TX